NUGGETS FOR RAISING GODLY CHILDREN

Helping parents-to-be, parents, grandparents and guardians bring up their children in a godly way in this sinful generation (Proverbs 22:6).

ISRAEL PHILIP

COVENANT PUBLISHING

Nuggets For Raising Godly Children
Israel Philip

Unless otherwise indicated, all scripture quotations are taken from King James Version (KJV) of the Bible.

ISBN 978-1-907734-42-7
First E-book Edition, May 2019

No part of this publication may be produced, distorted or transmitted in any form or by any means, including photocopying, recording or other electronic or mechanical methods, without the prior written permission of the publisher, or except in the case of brief quotations embodied in critical reviews and certain other non-commercial uses permitted by copyright law.

For permission requests, write to the publisher, addressed "Attention: Permission Coordinator" at the email address:

samadewunmi@btinternet.com

Copyright © May 2019, Israel Philip

Cover Design by Covenant Publishing Team
Published by Covenant Publishing
Printed in the United Kingdom

TABLE OF CONTENTS

Dedication	v
Acknowledgements	vii
Endorsements	xi
Foreword	xiii
Introduction	15
Nugget 1	
Pray For Unborn Children	19
Nugget 2	
Give Your Children Godly Names	23
Nugget 3	
Pray Ceaselessly For Your Children	29
Nugget 4	
Pray with Your Children	35
Nugget 5	
Speak To Your Children About God	41
Nugget 6	
Bring Them To Church	45
Nugget 7	
Build Their Faith	47
Nugget 8	
Model Giving to God And Humanity	49
Nugget 9	
Encourage Godly Service	53
Nugget 10	
Hold Family Meetings	59
Nugget 11	
Be In Control Of Your Home	63
Nugget 12	
Teach Forgiveness To Your Children	67

Nugget 13
Be Your Child's Best Friend — 71
Nugget 14
Build Their Self-Esteem — 75
Nugget 15
Create Their World By Your Words — 79
Nugget 16
Motivate Them To Aim High — 83
Nugget 17
Be The Shepherd And Not The Bull — 89
Nugget 18
Leave The Inheritance Inside Your Children — 93
Nugget 19
Teach About Financial Intelligence — 99
Nugget 20
Teach Them To Cook — 103
Nugget 21
Love Your Children Unconditionally — 107
Nugget 22
Discipline And Correct Your Children In Love — 111
Nugget 23
'NO' Is A Godly Answer — 117
Nugget 24
Keep Them Always Before The Throne — 121
Nugget 25
Pray For Your Future In-Laws — 125
About The Book — **127**
About The Author — **129**

DEDICATION

Nuggets for Raising Godly Children is dedicated to the memory of my loving mother, Mrs Beatrice Philip Ejiofor Ugwoemaju, who single-handedly loved, nurtured and raised me from Primary to Secondary school. She also sponsored my business which brought me to where I am today.

The book is also dedicated to all single parents that circumstances have made them to train their children alone. I want to assure you that you are not alone. God is with you in this journey, and He will see you through.

I want to dedicate this book mostly to all the Parents, Grand Parents and Guardian who are doing their very best to raise their children and grandchildren in the way of the Lord. Our God will crown all your effort with success.

Finally, I want to dedicate this book to all who make every effort to bring their children to church and to Sunday School to learn about the way of the Lord in this heartless, sinful and adulterous generation. Your labour in the Lord will not be in vain in Jesus name, Amen.

ACKNOWLEDGEMENTS

My first acknowledgement and thanks go to my Father in heaven who has been and remains my father forever since my biological father Mr Philip Ejiofor Ugwoemaju passed away in 1973 when I was barely four years old, whom through His grace and mercy the vision of this book was birthed. I thank Him also who considered the situation of this generation which has deteriorated into ungodliness amongst the younger generation that it is now vital for this book to be birthed.

I want to appreciate my peaceful wife Peace and our three lovely children; Favour, Prince-Joseph and Israel Junior for your love, support and encouragement throughout the time it took me to prepare this book. Thank you for all your prayers and God richly bless you.

I want to express my sincere appreciation and thanks to my Bishop and his lovely wife, Rev and Mrs Sam and Sofie Larbie for all your prayers and encouragement. Your words of advice by the grace of God always inspire me. Thank you also for choosing me as the Sunday School Superintendent of the Camberwell group of churches which gave me the platform to have some of the experiences that formed part of this book. God richly bless you sir and ma.

I want to thank our team of Pastors and congregation of the Right Now Jesus Centre Elim Church and The River of Life Centre Harlesden for all your support and prayers. The godly leadership we enjoy is amazing through which this book has become a reality; thank you so much and keep up the good work.

My sincere thanks go to Mama Joyce Tonto, the Sunday School, the Teachers, Supporters and the children. Every one of you in one way or the other have inspired me in the writing of this book and making the vision a reality.

I want to appreciate the entire congregation of Elim Pentecostal Church Camberwell and branches, all the pastors and your members for your unreserved support and encouragement in making this vision a reality. God bless you richly.

I want to appreciate the Senior Pastor of The Likewise Christian Ministries, his wife, the pastors and the entire congregation, for your encouragement and support throughout my pastoral training in your church. Whilst training, your Church became our second home church. Thank you so much for all the love demonstrated to my entire family. God richly bless you all.

My special thanks go to Sister Yemisi Feberesima and the entire hospitality team for inspiring me in a special way to birth this book. God bless you all and keep up the good work.

I want to finally thank my Umuozu family, my in-laws Amankuta, my family friends, brethren at work fellowship, friends, and well-wishers who have contributed in one way or another to my life and ministry journey and to the cultivation and birthing of this vision. May our good Lord bless you all immensely even as you read and apply the principles in this book in Jesus name, Amen.

x

ENDORSEMENTS

The nuggets of parenting explored in this book remain relevant and generational, coming from a place of experience and inspiration from the Holy Spirit. It covers most areas of life, seasons of development providing practical and tangible guidelines centred on prayers, hope and rewards. It is a must read for those on this journey of parenting in the varied capacities and others yet to join this God-given race.

Mrs Yemisi Fiberesima

Knife crime is on the rise in today's UK. Children are poorly motivated and ill-prepared for adult life. They are growing to become angry and bitter against anyone and everyone and parents and the authorities, in exasperation and utter resignation, have called them a wasted generation.

It's into this mess and foreboding that Pastor Israel Philip steps in with a ray of hope through this book. As a Sunday School teacher and superintendent, well known to me for more than two decades, he has methodically proffered solutions as he takes us through an odyssey of self-realisation.

I recommend this book to everyone who has hope for a better tomorrow for the next generation.

Pastor Fred Johnson-Esiri
Elim Church. Catford. South London

FOREWORD

Nuggets are rare to find. These are no rules or regulations that must be complied with. To ignore them will mean a loss in the final analysis.

I appointed pastor Israel Phillip as Sunday school superintendent of the Elim Pentecostal Church in Camberwell now known as the Right Now Jesus Centre in Lewisham London. The gentle application of the nuggets in question to the Sunday School department released a slow but progressive transformation to the Sunday School. He included careers planning day where professionals spoke to the kids dressed in their professional attire to reflect what you do in life. We have had representations cutting across many professions such as police officers, professional teachers, and ministers of religion, and medical doctors, and professional footballers, officers from the Fire service, probationary officers and many others. Through these encounters, the kids have thrived and grown confidently in this environment, of which Pastor Israel established. I have seen babies born in this church and develop through Sunday school and become wonderful people. After thirteen to fourteen years, they graduate into the youth church. It is a vital process in the life of this church.

I am very proud of the Sunday School Superintendent and the entire staff. I appreciate parents and guardians who have cooperated with the Sunday School over the years.

This is a must-read book, and I seriously recommend it to relatives and friends. Learning to say no without feeling guilty is a significant virtue of life.

Pastor Sam Larbie
Senior Pastor Right Now Jesus Centre

INTRODUCTION

This book is for parents-to-be, parents, grandparents and guardian of children.

The book is a simple piece which is to serve as a guide to raising godly children in this sinful world. It may be that you are preparing to be a parent, or you are a parent, grandparent, great grandparent or guardian of children, this book is intended to guide you in this journey of bringing up or raising these precious children the good Lord has blessed you with, in a godly way.

The advice and instructions given in this book are intended only as a guide; it may not necessarily be rigidly followed to bring about some desired results. Just as our Lord Jesus Christ is our ultimate healer, He also uses doctors to prescribe diverse medicines for the healing of various deceases. So it is in raising godly children. God, the Holy Spirit, is the ultimate teacher and guardian in life. His teachings and guidance are always the best.

Some children may rebel when you begin to apply the principles highlighted in this book. Ultimately, they will come back according to the scripture.

> *"Train up a child in the way he should go: and when he is old, he will not depart from it" (Proverbs 22:6).*

Life is about faith. You need to have faith in God to accomplish this enormous task of raising your children in a godly way. So, when they grow up, they will not depart from the Lord. I heard a story of the son a certain great man of God. This man pastors a large congregation which comprises of both young and old, but his son was a rebel who lived a different lifestyle. The young man in question smoked weeds (Class B drugs according to UK drug law). This boy lived away from his parents and lived with a girlfriend. One day his brother visited him and knocked on the door. When his girlfriend opened the door, everywhere was covered with the smell of weed. It is very disheartening that this great man of God raised him with all the Christian values, ethics and attributes yet he decided to live like the prodigal son. But guess what, every prodigal son or daughter must one day come to their senses. The boy in question later returned to his father and to the Lord Who has now called him into full-time ministry as a Pastor of a church.

The Biblical story of the prodigal son is a typical example.

> *"And he said, 'A certain man had two sons: and the younger of them said to his father, Father, give me the portion of goods that falleth to me. And he divided unto them his living. And not many days after the younger son gathered all together, and took his journey into a far country, and there wasted*

his substance with riotous living. And when he had spent all, there arose a mighty famine in that land; and he began to be in want. And he went and joined himself to a citizen of that country; and he sent him into his fields to feed swine. And he would fain have filled his belly with the husks that the swine did eat: and no man gave unto him. And when he came to himself, he said, How many hired servants of my father's have bread enough and to spare, and I perish with hunger! I will arise and go to my father, and will say unto him, Father, I have sinned against heaven, and before thee, and am no more worthy to be called thy son: make me as one of thy hired servants. And he arose and came to his father. But when he was yet a great way off, his father saw him, and had compassion, and ran, and fell on his neck, and kissed him. And the son said unto him, Father, I have sinned against heaven, and in thy sight, and am no more worthy to be called thy son. But the father said to his servants, Bring forth the best robe, and put it on him; and put a ring on his hand, and shoes on his feet: And bring hither the fatted calf, and kill it; and let us eat, and be merry: For this my son was dead, and is alive again; he was lost, and is found. And they began to be merry" (Luke 15:11-24).

One critical step for any parent whose son or daughter is out as a prodigal is to keep praying for them, and never confess negative about them. Pray that the good Lord will protect and preserve them from the wolves out there. Keep expecting their return and trusting them into the hands of our good Lord for protection.

As you have fulfilled your responsibility by bringing them up in the way they should go, when they are old, they will not depart from it. There is an excellent result in both raising a child in the way they should go and continually praying for them even while they are there in the prodigal land. Not giving up and not giving in to the negativity of the enemy is vital in winning the battle you and your children are together engaged. Maybe they are in prison or out there in the prodigal wilderness, keep praying for them and never give up.

NUGGET 1

PRAY FOR UNBORN CHILDREN

An excellent nugget to start with is that you should pray for your unborn children.

Today maybe, you have not yet been blessed with having children, I will encourage you to start praying for your future children. Call them by name (if you already know their names) and pray that the God that makes the impossibilities possible, will bring them to pass in your life and the life of your family in Jesus name, Amen. Before I had my children, even before my wife came over to the UK and we got married, I have already named all our children and have been praying for them by their names as I do now that I have received them from God.

> *"Lo, children are an heritage of the Lord: and the fruit of the womb is his reward. As*

> *arrows are in the hand of a mighty man; so are children of the youth. Happy is the man that hath his quiver full of them: they shall not be ashamed, but they shall speak with the enemies in the gate" (Psalms 127:3-5).*

Today, to the glory of God, He has given us our three children, and I have continued to pray for them and will continue to pray for them until I leave this world to go back to my Father in heaven.

Prayer never stops. First, I listed their names, and weekly, I prayed for them mentioning their names during the prayers.

> *"As it is written, I have made thee a father of many nations, before him whom he believed, even God, who quickeneth the dead, and calleth those things which be not as though they were. Who against hope believed in hope, that he might become the father of many nations; according to that which was spoken, So shall thy seed be. And being not weak in faith, he considered not his own body now dead, when he was about an hundred years old, neither yet the deadness of Sara's womb" (Romans 4:17-19).*

Prayer and faith work together, for you cannot pray without faith. Raising children with Christian values is an act of faith.

> *"But without faith it is impossible to please him: for he that cometh to God must believe*

that he is, and that he is a rewarder of them that diligently seek him" (Hebrews 11:6).

Your part of the bargain is to pray with faith while God's role is to answer your prayers. All that the good Lord needs from you is a little faith. Just a little faith is enough for Him to do wonders in your life and your family. If you have ever seen a mustard seed, you would have understood better what the Lord meant by just a little faith.

"And the Lord said, If ye had faith as a grain of mustard seed, ye might say unto this sycamore tree, Be thou plucked up by the root, and be thou planted in the sea; and it should obey you" (Luke 17:6).

Pray Into Your Children's Life

From the moment a child is conceived inside the mother's womb, that child requires prayers. The first two weeks to one month are vital especially for those households who have been waiting upon the Lord for their blessings or those going through the challenges of miscarriages. You pray into that baby's life whether a boy or a girl. That very moment, praying is to sustain the baby by the grace of God. It may not happen to everybody the same way, but I pray that everyone reading this book at this moment who is having miscarriages, the next conception will not miscarry in the mighty name of Jesus, Amen.

Prayer Works. If you believe it, say it in prayers, and our good Lord will answer you and change your story. From conception, you must pray until your baby is born. This means the first stage of the battle is won. Remember that not everyone who ever conceived a baby was able to deliver. So, if God in His mercy granted you grace to conceive and carry you throughout pregnancy and you delivered peacefully, you need to be thankful to Him. The enemy always works so hard to terminate babies from the womb, but the intervention from above saves them and the mother also.

The journey has now begun, you need to keep praying for that baby according to the way the good Lord has blessed you. You will need to pray until that child starts crawling, pray for protection and smooth development. Soon the baby will start 'toothing' with changes in temperature and mood plus sleepless nights, all start at the same time. You need to be praying as the child grows. If your child has cold especially your first child, the nose blocks, the child struggled to breathe, you think the child will not make it through, but prayers at that time goes a long way to not only heal the child but also to increase your faith in God's power to heal the sick. Starting from your family, if your child's cold leaves and he or she gets healed as a result of your faith and your prayers, then you will be able to go out there with that same faith to pray for others.

NUGGET 2

GIVE YOUR CHILDREN GODLY NAMES

Names are significant and should be taken seriously. Some parents do not prayerfully name their children. Even before the child is born, at least two names should be waiting for the baby, be it a boy or a girl.

> *"And he said, Let me go, for the day breaketh. And he said, I will not let thee go, except thou bless me. And he said unto him, What is thy name? And he said, Jacob. And he said, Thy name shall be called no more Jacob, but Israel: for as a prince hast thou power with God and with men, and hast prevailed. And Jacob asked him, and said, Tell me, I pray thee, thy name. And he said, Wherefore is it that thou dost ask after my*

name? And he blessed him there" (Genesis 32:26-29).

God through His Angel changed Jacob to Israel with its meaning. God changed Abram to Abraham. He also renamed Sarai to Sarah. All of these have powerful meaning. All the covenanted names in the Bible have meanings. I do also know that so many give names to their children based on their circumstances. Can I please advise that you do not make a permanent decision based on a temporary condition. If you give your child a name based on what you are going through which may be a brief challenge, then you must remember that the name is permanent. Please do take time and pray before you give your children names. Do give your children positive, beautiful, lovely, and meaningful names which as they are called, blessings are being released on them. You are known by your name. So every name you give to your child is like a pronouncement which people will be making on that child all the days of his or her life. So please do take your time and pray about it. Check the meaning of that name so that you know, as people call him or her that name, they are either praying for that child or prophesying to the child. Don't just wake up and think about your enemy and give your child a name to reflect your enmity with your next-door neighbour or someone else in the neighbourhood or even family issues or family conflicts. Do not give your child a name that has no meaning or naming your child after your parents when you know their names has no meaning.

Do not copy others like friends or neighbours, because things will change, and people will move to different directions in life. Do not reflect your present situation which is temporary on the children God has given to you. I happen to come from the part of the world where names play a significant role in life, and we do not joke with names. My father gave his children meaningful names from the Bible; names like, "Godspower", "ThankGod", and "Godwin", including my very own name, "Israel." Naming your child is a very important delegated responsibility. As parents, God gave the children to us and commissioned us to name them. The responsibility is transferable. As you name your children, so will they name their own children. Some parents have been privileged to name their grandchildren. Naming the children should be excellently executed any time we have the privilege to do so. Do not allow social media to decide the name of your children. Do not allow trends or style of things to influence your decision. Remember, all these are temporary circumstances which will come to pass, but your child is a permanent gift from God who will stay with you forever.

Prayer Puts You At Peace

Praying for your children is very important because when you pray, you put God to work by handing over everything to him. He said,

> *"Ask, and it shall be given you; seek, and ye shall find; knock, and it shall be opened unto you: For every one that asketh receiveth; and he that seeketh findeth; and to him that knocketh it shall be opened" (Matthew 7:7-8).*

In asking, there are no situations, especially when it concerns our children that can be too big or too small for our God to handle. Sometimes, we choose the ones we like and think God may not be bothered about the others. God cares about even the minute part of our concerns, not to talk of our children who are precious before Him. God's power to deliver is so great to the point of that hopeless situation. Wait a moment, who has the final say over your life and your case? Is it not JEHOVAH? So please bring it all to Him in prayer.

I do have absolute confidence that He will resolve it all and give you victory. Remember, it is not yet over until God says so. Your child may be in prison of any kind; may be physical, mental, emotional or even financial prison, just pray and put your trust in God for His redemptive power to overcome. I know without any shadow of a doubt that He will never fail. He has never failed, and He will never change because you are His child.

A Christian woman met a great man of God at a convention. This woman raised his son as a Christian young man, but he derailed out of faith. One day, he got arrested for murder which he did not commit. It was a case of mistaken identity and he was facing death by hanging. The mum visited him in prison and questioned if he indeed committed the crime. He told the mum he did not commit this crime. Her mother believed him knowing that her son will never lie to her. May I quickly point out that trust was already built in the mother-son relationship. It is vital as parents to trust your child and for your child always to tell you the absolute truth. This woman came to the convention that night knowing that her son will be hanged by midnight if God did not step in. She stepped forward to this great man of God and requested that he prayed so that her son will not to be hanged for the crime he did not commit. The man of God agreed with her that her son would not be killed. To the glory of God, just before midnight, the culprit telephoned the police officer-in-charge, admitting to the crime and the woman's son was set free.

I do not know your situation as you read this book; just lay your hand on this page and declare that the God that answered this woman at her critical time of need should answer you in Jesus name, Amen.

Nuggets For Raising Godly Children

NUGGET 3

PRAY CEASELESSLY FOR YOUR CHILDREN

You should pray ceaselessly for your children.

"Pray without season" (1 Thessalonians 5:17)

Prayer is communication with God Almighty. In this context, you are not only talking to God about your children, God can speak to you about them at the same time. The most important thing you can do for your children is to pray for them, pray into their life, pray into their destiny, and pray into their future, not just to feed and clothe them. You never know what God has in store for that little child in your hand. Do not underestimate what God can do in the life of any child be they male or female.

Being in the children ministry for a considerable length of time has thought me a lot of lessons about children, I have seen children born and dedicated into the church via children ministry, grow up, graduate from Sunday School and progress through the state-run school system (Nursery, Primary, Secondary, College), finish University, get a good job, get married, have their own children and brought them to the Sunday School ministry they attended. There goes the cycle. Most of all, I have seen them fulfil their dreams and visions in life and in the various ministries God has called them, and I marvel at the mighty handy work of God.

> *"Be careful for nothing; but in everything by prayer and supplication with thanksgiving let your requests be made known unto God" (Philippians 4:6).*

> *"O Lord, rebuke me not in thine anger, neither chasten me in thy hot displeasure" (Psalms 6:1).*

> *"If thy people go out to battle against their enemy, whithersoever thou shalt send them, and shall pray unto the Lord toward the city which thou hast chosen, and toward the house that I have built for thy name: Then hear thou in heaven their prayer and their supplication, and maintain their cause. If they sin against thee, (for there is no man that sinneth not) and thou be angry with them, and deliver them to the enemy, so that they carry them away captives unto the land*

of the enemy, far or near; Yet if they shall bethink themselves in the land whither they were carried captives, and repent, and make supplication unto thee in the land of them that carried them captives, saying, We have sinned, and have done perversely, we have committed wickedness; And so return unto thee with all their heart, and with all their soul, in the land of their enemies, which led them away captive, and pray unto thee toward their land, which thou gavest unto their fathers, the city which thou hast chosen, and the house which I have built for thy name: Then hear thou their prayer and their supplication in heaven thy dwelling place, and maintain their cause, And forgive thy people that have sinned against thee, and all their transgressions wherein they have transgressed against thee, and give them compassion before them who carried them captive, that they may have compassion on them: For they be thy people, and thine inheritance, which thou broughtest forth out of Egypt, from the midst of the furnace of iron" (1 Kings 8:44-51).

These scriptures and many others present clear evidence that God answers prayers. He promised us that when we pray, He will hear us, and when it concerns our children and His children, He will answer us.

One songwriter described prayer as the master key that opens every door. Solomon prayed,

> *"If I shut up heaven that there be no rain, or if I command the locusts to devour the land, or if I send pestilence among my people; If my people, which are called by my name, shall humble themselves, and pray, and seek my face, and turn from their wicked ways; then will I hear from heaven, and will forgive their sin, and will heal their land"* (2 Chronicles 7:13-14).

Solomon prayed that if we, the people of God, should sin and ask for forgiveness, that our God should forgive us and deliver us and heal our land. Such prayers should always be said for our children. In fact, all situations and circumstances could be resolved through prayers. No condition can withstand the power of prayers; no demon, nor evil powers can stand the power of prayers. No stubbornness nor waywardness can resist the power of prayers. Either evil or wickedness; none can withstand the force of prayers.

In your prayers, the blood of Jesus Christ is a protective shield while the fire of the Holy Ghost is a consuming fire. Our enemies cannot withstand any of them. When you plead the blood of Jesus over your family (which are yourself and your children), they are covered; no matter where they are. When you send the Holy Ghost on a mission, the consuming fire will consume as instructed depending on the authority of the believer.

Prayers play a vital role in the life of every child, and that is why prayer is the most important gift any parent or guardian can give to their children. There are no limits to prayers, no special time nor season for prayers and most of all no special place for prayers. Prayers could be said anytime and anywhere for your children. It is important to pray for your children because their future is in the hands of the Almighty God.

> *"So then it is not of him that willeth, nor of him that runneth, but of God that sheweth mercy" (Romans 9:16).*

Prayer is the only force that can destroy the devil's plan and destabilise and put confusion in his kingdom. Prayers can bind all the operations of the wicked world and their demonic agents and suspend their activities.

> *"For we wrestle not against flesh and blood, but against principalities, against powers, against the rulers of the darkness of this world, against spiritual wickedness in high places. Wherefore take unto you the whole armour of God, that ye may be able to withstand in the evil day, and having done all, to stand" (Ephesians 6:12-13).*

> *"For the weapons of our warfare are not carnal, but mighty through God to the pulling down of strongholds, Casting down imaginations, and every high thing that exalteth itself against the knowledge of God, and bringing into captivity every thought to the obedience of Christ" (2 Corinthians 10:4-5).*

Nuggets For Raising Godly Children

NUGGET 4

PRAY WITH YOUR CHILDREN

Praying with your children is very important, and it plays two significant roles in raising godly children. First, when you pray with them, you are committing them into the hand of God, and second, you are also teaching them how to pray.

Children are always copying their parents. That is why the children of most parents who smoke cigarette end up smoking as well. They copy their parents. A proverb from my home country said: "As the mother sheep is eating yam, the little one is watching the mouth". The reason is that the little one will soon start eating like the mother. Children always copy their parents, and this is highly commended especially when it involves praying together.

Praying for others with your children encourages your children to have a sense of care and support. Through prayers for others and God answering your prayers, the children are challenged by the awesomeness of God's goodness, and they could see through what God has done that He is good and that His mercies endure forever. When you experience answered prayers, most times it draws difficult children back to God. Therefore, it is paramount that we exercise our spiritual authority. When God answers our prayers regarding our children, everybody will be happy including our children and that will confirm the saying that "when you work, you work, but when you pray, you ask God to work on your behalf".

When you pray with your children, you are teaching your children the best thing in life; that part of life is showing them the way to God. When you pray with them, you are teaching them how to fight their spiritual battles. This is so important because they will graduate to the point of doing it themselves; may be at the University Campus, at a time they are on their own, far away from Mummy and Daddy or Grandad and Grandma. They will remember all the prayers you prayed together. You may be surprised the next time you hear him or her praying; you think it's yourself. Because they have copied you and by watching you pray, they are now reaching to our God on their own.

There is no better way of teaching your children the best way in life than to show by example when you pray with them. My mum started praying with me when I was very young. I still remember when she knelt at her bed side to call upon JEHOVAH. I subsequently copied my mums' prayers and gradually started adding my own words.

The starting point is vital. So many people want to do something good but struggle to make a start. I challenge you to be an example to your children. As soon as they have a great start, they will continue and will never stop. At some point in life, they will face the realities of life, then your input into their life will manifest. No matter how short the prayer is, our God honours it. God does not answer prayers based on the length of time spend talking to Him about our needs. Instead, He answers prayers by His grace through His word.

> *"If my people, which are called by my name, shall humble themselves, and pray, and seek my face, and turn from their wicked ways; then will I hear from heaven, and will forgive their sin, and will heal their land"* (2 Chronicles 7:14).

Teach Them To Pray

The saying that children do not only do what you instruct them to do, but they do what they watch you do is correct in some aspect, and the issue of prayer and faith are two examples. The way to teach your children how to pray is to pray with them. As they watch you model, conduct the prayer, and intercede for yourself and others, it will make them understand that they need to pray for themselves and others as well. Teaching your children how to pray is done by example. For instance, if I tell my children to go and pray, being children, they may get upstairs and start either playing or fighting over one thing or the other and never pray. But if I say to them, let us go upstairs and pray, they will all follow me, and we will all go and have our prayers whether morning prayers or night prayers and while we are doing that, we are fulfilling scripture.

> *"Train up a child in the way he should go: and when he is old, he will not depart from it" (Proverbs 22:6).*

Prayer Is A Transferable Behaviour

Praying with your children is a contagious and transferable behaviour which your children can then transfer to their children. Those among us who are blessed with grandchildren, please let your grandchildren learn these behaviours, especially when they come over for a holiday, weekend or sleepover. Do not go inside your room to pray alone, no! Please pray with them thereby teaching them how to pray and communicate with our heavenly father. I must tell you that this very singular act of prayer will be a memorial for you when you have been called home to be with Jesus. They will not only remember you always pray with them but that you also carry on the same legacy of praying with them and your grandchildren. The grandchildren will tell their children the story of how they always visit grandma and grandpa, and before bed or in the morning grandma and grandpa still call them out for either night prayers or morning devotion. Some children will love it, and it may be the only reason they to go to their grandparent's house.

Teaching our children to pray by example is the most effective way of bringing up our children in the way of the Lord. In other words, we are saying to our children that whatever you need in life, you need to go to God in prayers and He will hear and answer all the unspeakable request of your heart. The scripture said that our God knows our needs and have our good intention at heart, and most especially His plans for us are plans of good and not of evil.

> *"For I know the thoughts that I think toward you, saith the Lord, thoughts of peace, and not of evil, to give you an expected end. Then shall ye call upon me, and ye shall go and pray unto me, and I will hearken unto you. And ye shall seek me, and find me, when ye shall search for me with all your heart"* (Jeremiah 29:11-13).

Our good God will bring these good plans to fruition as we put our complete trust in Him in the life our children in Jesus name, Amen.

Nuggets For Raising Godly Children

NUGGET 5

SPEAK TO YOUR CHILDREN ABOUT GOD

Telling your children about all aspect of God is vital. He is merciful. He is powerful. He is loving, yet He is a consuming fire. He rewards generational blessing and punishes from generation to generation.

The story of Prophet Eli is a typical example. The children possibly did not understand God's other side. Even when God warned Eli of the impending doom and what He was about to do to the whole household as a result of the action of Eli's children, he still did not warn them of the impending consequences. This is also the case of some of us today; we are not warning our children about the impending consequences of their actions.

Some parents will see their teenage children out and about in the night and not be bothered. After school, instead of coming home to study, they are out on the street loitering. Some come back with a strange bag hanging across their neck. We do need to check the bag as to know what is inside; maybe there is a knife or even a gun. If something unusual is discovered, we do need to rebuke them, making them understand the consequences of the steps they are taking.

Telling them about God and what God can do is vital. Maybe they are going through a phase in their lives but are uncomfortable to talk about it; you can encourage them and help them find a solution. In major cities of the world and especially in London, teenagers are killed daily. Most of them are killed because they do not understand the consequences of their actions, which has resulted in their becoming prematurely killed by rival gang members. Some of them are murdered for revenge of what the gang member did to the other gang. Some innocent teenagers are killed as a result of being at the wrong place, at the wrong time. These children do know the law of the land, but they do not know the law of God, nor do they understand who God is. Knowing that the life they took was not theirs and it neither belongs to the government, but instead, it belongs to God, will bring them to understand who God is and what He can do. The scripture said, do not fear the one who will kill this body and cannot do anything else.

"And I say unto you my friends, Be not afraid of them that kill the body, and after that have no more that they can do. But I will forewarn you whom ye shall fear: Fear him, which after he hath killed hath power to cast into hell; yea, I say unto you, Fear him" (Luke 12:4-5).

God has the power not only to kill but also to cast into hell.

To the parents of young teenage girls; when you see your girl not returning from school at the right time, going out and staying out late and returning with various excuses, it is time for you to call your beloved girl in for a chat. It's time for correction and time to teach your girl about our loving God. Knowing that, if a negative result comes out of the late nights and late return from school, then you did warn her. Unchecked late night returns and continued lack of discipline has most times resulted in teenage pregnancies, which brings shame to the family and the church of God. This complicates the system in the sense that the fathers and mothers of the babies are still children. They do not understand the concept of raising children because they are children themselves, under parental care, or even attending college or university. What can you say? No proper job, no regular income.

As a parent, you need to take time out to tell your children the consequences of every unacceptable behaviour you notice so that they will take precaution and refrain from them. Do not wait until they do something stupid before you start blaming them for putting you to shame. Drive that shame far from you by talking to your children about the love of God. Some parents have suddenly become grandparents unprepared because their children got pregnant and gave birth out of wedlock. It is not a thing to be proud of because you did not raise your children in that manner. You want to plan and execute the wedding of your children and send them off to their marital home, but when the reverse is the case, you have no choice than to accept your fortune.

Remember, even in such circumstances, do not give up on your children. Keep talking to God about them and keep talking to them about God. None of this cycle will stop; instead, it is a continuous process. One thing is very clear; if it goes well, you will enjoy it, and if it goes wrong, you will also be there for them. But we pray that all our children will listen to us and make the right decision so that it will be well with us all. No matter the situation, please do not give up on your children.

NUGGET 6

BRING THEM TO CHURCH

Bringing your children to Christ and to church is a foundational job of the parents. As you know, the foundation of every building determines the height and size of the building.

Raising your children in a godly way is a decision you make in your heart and agree with your spouse. That is the first and the most critical step of raising your children. After this has been agreed with your spouse, you will follow it up by taking your children to the church daily, which is a huge sacrifice but very rewarding in the end. You will need to pray for them always and pray with them also in order to teach them how to pray. You will need to read and teach them Gods word, for this is called the bread of life. Understanding your children is paramount in the parenting journey. As you carry on raising your children, if you notice them having low self-esteem, please do not ignore it. Talk to them and talk to someone, possibly a professional, to help at that very moment.

There are so much to learn from our parents, grandparents and guardian, especially godly parents. Those who are patient with their children and who stick together to do the right thing even when it is not convenient for them. Those who do their best to take their children to church every Sunday morning, so that they will hear and learn the word of God and the way of Salvation. You cannot underestimate the blessing of taking your children to church every Sunday. As a Sunday School teacher for the past twenty years, I have seen and had loads of experience regarding bringing your children to church to learn the word of God from the Sunday School teachers.

It is profitable to bring your young children to the feet of Christ so that when they are old, they will not depart from God's way. The word of God is a seed. That is why it is essential to bring your children to church in order for the foundation to be laid. When a child whose foundation was laid in Sunday School grows, they will never depart from what they were taught as they start life. Things like; obedience to the authorities and the words of God, prayers for yourself and others, giving to God and other people, reading and obeying God's Word

NUGGET 7

BUILD THEIR FAITH

This is how faith is built; you start from little and then go to big faith. Parents are the priest of the house as far as the children are concerned.

> *"But ye are a chosen generation, a royal priesthood, an holy nation, a peculiar people; that ye should shew forth the praises of him who hath called you out of darkness into his marvellous light"* (1 Peter 2:9).

This Scripture is made manifest starting from your home, where you are the first priest your children know. Only when it becomes tough that you will seek the help of your Pastor or Priest or even your Bishop. You must first of all deal with it when it is small, and even when the big one comes, you will be expected to handle it.

> *"And the Lord said, If ye had faith as a grain of mustard seed, ye might say unto this sycamore tree, Be thou plucked up by the root, and be thou planted in the sea; and it should obey you" (Luke 17:6).*

Our God honours faith; no matter how little. Faith is the currency through which we can purchase anything from the Throne of God.

> *"But without faith it is impossible to please him: for he that cometh to God must believe that he is, and that he is a rewarder of them that diligently seek him" (Hebrews 11:6).*

Our God can only be impressed by faith; therefore as parents, you need to build your faith enough to take care of your own family. Faith is infectious. That means if you are a person of faith, your children will pick up from you and build their faith from yours. I picked up from the faith of my mother, Mrs Beatrice Philip Ugwoamaju, of blessed memory. She singlehandedly raised me by the grace of God. My dad, Mr Philip Ejiofor Ugoamaju, went to be with the Lord when I was just four years old. As her last baby, my mum took care of me and guided me in the way of the Lord. I copied my mum's prayer style, and that was how I started praying on my own. When I became of age, my mum bought me my first Bible to start my life unknown to her that our God was using her to prepare me as a vessel for the propagation of the gospel of the Kingdom of God.

NUGGET 8

MODEL GIVING TO GOD AND HUMANITY

Giving is a godly principle and is one of the secrets of prosperity and increase. The word of God says in Luke 6:38,

> *"Give, and it shall be given unto you; good measure, pressed down, and shaken together, and running over, shall men give into your bosom. For with the same measure that ye mete withal it shall be measured to you again."*

The same principle in reverse means, if you do not give, nothing will come back to you. Every form of giving is an attribute of sowing a seed. As we all know that you cannot reap if you did not sow, who will sow what you will reap? Therefore, sowing is the only step you take if you want to reap a harvest.

Harvest is essential in life. If you have no harvest, it means there is nothing to live on. If you do not sow, how can you reap? So please try to teach your children how to sow by example. Try always to give them money for offering in the church. Try to include them whenever you are giving any charitable gift. They may out of curiosity ask you what you are doing. Use that opportunity to educate them.

Teach them Where, When, How and What to sow. As we parents know, there are factors that contribute to great harvest. They are the above mentioned. The ground you sow your seed most times determines your harvest. Sowing on good ground is vital and can contribute to a great harvest. Therefore, we should guide our children into making sure the place they are putting their seed will bring great result.

The season you sow is another determining factor to your great harvest.

> *"To everything there is a season, and a time to every purpose under the heaven" (Ecclesiastes 3:1).*

You cannot plant a seed at a very wrong time and expect a great harvest. Sometimes even the seed will die without germinating. The state of your mind when you sow your seed also will determine the type of harvest you will reap.

> *"Every man according as he purposeth in his heart, so let him give; not grudgingly, or of*

necessity: for God loveth a cheerful giver" (*2 Corinthians 9:7*).

Teach your children to sow a worthy seed, not leftovers, loose change, or rejected products like that of Cain. Our God is not a beggar. He owns the whole world, and everything belongs to Him. When you give to God, you are opening doors for your blessings. God is always looking for an opportunity to bless His children. In our giving, we open the doors of blessings and prosperity for our children and us. In life, we sow every day; in the morning and the day and the night, you sow for yourself and others.

One of the things you sow is prayers. You sow prayer for self and to others. Anytime you say prayers for yourself and others, the Holy Spirit of God takes over, guides and lead you all through the day. Sowing prayers for yourself, your family and others are vital. It is like buying insurance for yourself and your family and helping your loved ones have the same protection. You do not wait for an accident to happen before you buy insurance, otherwise, you will not be protected, but you buy insurance early. In case of accident or incident, the insurance company will pay out, and that will replace any lost or damaged property. Please always say prayers for self and your family. Pray for your minister of God, and pray for those in authority.

Nuggets For Raising Godly Children

NUGGET 9

ENCOURAGE GODLY SERVICE

Teach your children to sow money and their talent in the house of God and be humble

This nugget is slightly different from the previous one which primarily focused on the obedience to give back to God and to help the needy.

The substance you sow is fundamental. That is why it is essential for you to teach your children to sow their finance and their talent. Just as sowing prayers is significant at the beginning of each day's journey, so also is teaching your children the importance of giving to the house God when they are young. Sowing money can be in the form of tithe and offering, or through a pledge. When our children learn early in life the importance of tithe and offering, it enhances their knowledge and places them on the platform for success. This means that our children are starting early to make deposits into the kingdom of God even when they are using their talents as an investment in the house of God.

Sowing can be done in diverse ways. Sowing money is one way while your talent is another product you can sow to God and He will increase it for you.

Tithe and offering are paid in the church where you receive spiritual nourishment. In the same manner, God blesses our children with talents that can be used in the house of God to glorify His holy name. I tried to learn different types of musical instruments but did not succeed. I decided to join the music team but could not sing because that is not what God wants for me. But I encourage any child to learn both instruments and music. Success in either or both is as a result of God's gift plus hard work. I felt mine was not in that direction. If God has given you the privilege to do anything in the house of God, please do not brag or boast about it because it is a privilege. Many tried and could not succeed, but you are privileged. I will, therefore, encourage that you be humble and serve. That's where your blessings come from.

Do teach your children to be humble in all they do in life because pride goes before destruction.

> *"Pride goeth before destruction, and an haughty spirit before a fall. Better it is to be of an humble spirit with the lowly, than to*

divide the spoil with the proud" (Proverbs 16:18-19).

Every gift from God is given for a reason, just to use it to glorify the name of Jesus in the capacity you can, knowing that you were privileged to be given that grace by God. There is a parable of the talent in Matthew 25:14-30;

"For the kingdom of heaven is as a man travelling into a far country, who called his own servants, and delivered unto them his goods. And unto one he gave five talents, to another two, and to another one; to every man according to his several ability; and straightway took his journey. Then he that had received the five talents went and traded with the same, and made them other five talents. And likewise he that had received two, he also gained other two. But he that had received one went and digged in the earth, and hid his lord's money. After a long time the lord of those servants cometh, and reckoneth with them. And so he that had received five talents came and brought other five talents, saying, Lord, thou deliveredst unto me five talents: behold, I have gained beside them five talents more. His lord said unto him, Well done, thou good and faithful servant: thou hast been faithful over a few things, I will make thee ruler over many things: enter thou into the joy of thy lord. He also that had received two talents came and said, Lord, thou deliveredst unto me two

talents: behold, I have gained two other talents beside them. His lord said unto him, Well done, good and faithful servant; thou hast been faithful over a few things, I will make thee ruler over many things: enter thou into the joy of thy lord. Then he which had received the one talent came and said, Lord, I knew thee that thou art an hard man, reaping where thou hast not sown, and gathering where thou hast not strawed: And I was afraid, and went and hid thy talent in the earth: lo, there thou hast that is thine. His lord answered and said unto him, Thou wicked and slothful servant, thou knewest that I reap where I sowed not, and gather where I have not strawed: Thou oughtest therefore to have put my money to the exchangers, and then at my coming I should have received mine own with usury. Take therefore the talent from him, and give it unto him which hath ten talents. For unto every one that hath shall be given, and he shall have abundance: but from him that hath not shall be taken away even that which he hath. And cast ye the unprofitable servant into outer darkness: there shall be weeping and gnashing of teeth"

Money is also a gift from God whether to the believer or the unbeliever unless it was not genuine. Every genuine cash is a gift from God. So please let us use it and advise our children to use it to help people and glorify God who gave it to them.

"But thou shalt remember the Lord thy God: for it is he that giveth thee power to get wealth, that he may establish his covenant which he sware unto thy fathers, as it is this day" (Deuteronomy 8:18).

Please, parents, do teach your children all these in order to equip them for their future as they rely on Jesus the ultimate source of everything. Whenever there is an opportunity to give in the house of God, please encourage your children to give especially for the furtherance of the gospel.

Nuggets For Raising Godly Children

NUGGET 10
HOLD FAMILY MEETINGS

This may be new to you, but it is a significant activity that must be practised in every home. Maybe you are hearing about it for the first time, trust me, if you practice regular family meeting, you will have peace. Having regular family meetings with your children is vital because each time you have a meeting with them, it gives them the opportunity to express themselves, say what is in their minds and free themselves. It might not make sense at first, but give them the chance to speak their mind. Some of their contributions may not make sense now, but they will be glad they are given an opportunity to say something in the meeting. Parents should create an atmosphere of freedom of speech at the family meeting. The father or the mother may have the final say, but in a family meeting, you will be the coordinator at this time, give everyone a chance to talk and express themselves. In this family meeting, the parents should not be autocratic; you must be open to ideas for the family to move forward.

This meeting could be formal or informal; some may choose to hold it in the morning after morning prayers or in the evening but not when you or your children are tired which will not bring any fruit. Make it a very convenient time for everyone. Most times parents are too busy to have time together with the children, but on this occasion, please try and make out time for this is very important. Family meeting plays a significant role in building the confidence of your children in expressing themselves in public. At the family meeting, children are given the opportunity of expression. This also helps them to prepare for their future, attending meetings and making contributions and expressing themselves in public meetings.

In this meeting also you have the opportunity of guiding them on how to address and express themselves in a public meeting. Show them how sessions are run, what to do and when to do it. In organising this meeting at your house, you teach your children how to host meetings, and you too are learning because life is a learning Journey. Some of the agendas of this meeting will include appraisal and appreciation given to those that have done well and guidance and correction given to those who have not done well. This meeting time is an opportunity for new ideas that will uplift the entire family, new instruction that enables everyone to walk together, and raise concerns that have been ongoing but need to be addressed. It is at this meeting that order is restored and instructions are followed. You can also use this as an opportunity in giving and exchanging of gifts, as it is a time when families come together on their own for a good reason. Make sure the meeting end well if possible, with prayers at the beginning and the end. Do not allow the enemy to disrupt it and turn it into a time of quarrel or fight thereby disturb the peace of your family. Always end it positively because family comes first.

Nuggets For Raising Godly Children

NUGGET 11

BE IN CONTROL OF YOUR HOME

In the western world, this may sound a little out of place, but it is a reality, and it is achievable. For you to successfully raise your children in a godly way, you must first be in control. In a classroom as a Sunday school teacher for more than twenty years of both adult and children classes, it is difficult to teach a lesson if you are not really in control. The moment the children are out of control, you must bring them back under full control before you can be able to teach them the right way. In the same way, your children are your classroom sample. You have to be able to control them before leading them in the way of the Lord. No wonder some parents say, their children do not go to church again. It may be because they have lost control of their children or in other words they are out of control. By prayers and kind words, you can regain control of them. It is not good if your children are out of control and you are doing nothing about it just like Eli in the scripture. Even when the impending doom was revealed, he did nothing. Please make sure you do something when your children are out of control. Eli could have intercepted his children or scolded them or at least rebuked them, but he did not. The Bible did not record what action he took, only what he said.

> *"Then Eli called Samuel, and said, Samuel, my son. And he answered, Here am I. And he said, What is the thing that the Lord hath said unto thee? I pray thee hide it not from me: God do so to thee, and more also, if thou hide anything from me of all the things that he said unto thee. And Samuel told him every whit, and hid nothing from him. And he said, It is the Lord: let him do what seemeth him good" (1 Samuel 3:16-18).*

Their father lost control of those children to the point that when the Lord delivered that message of destruction to the whole family, the father could not do anything. In battle, the boys were destroyed, and the calamities fell on the entire family including Eli himself.

It is better that parents take control of their children while they are under their parental care. Do not allow them to take that control away from you and tell you what to do. If you allow them to take control of themselves at such tender age, the result is not always positive, and because they needed to be controlled but are not getting it at home, they will get it from the streets. The drug dealers will be controlling them with threats, and they will have no option than to surrender because the threat is real.

Many of such children are murdered in cold blood on the streets of UK, most times at midnight or early morning. Why would a teenager be outside by midnight in the street and doing what? We keep losing them daily, some as young as fourteen. Some do not have a home to go to and parents to listen to and even family to relax with.

Oh God, have mercy and parents, please take back control of the family, and for those who have wandered away, please pray for them daily and our merciful God will bring them back.

Nuggets For Raising Godly Children

NUGGET 12

TEACH FORGIVENENSS TO YOUR CHILDREN

"And forgive us our sins; for we also forgive every one that is indebted to us. And lead us not into temptation; but deliver us from evil" (Luke 11:4).

This scripture talks about the importance of forgiveness. The young generation needs to learn to forgive each other. Forgiveness, when instilled in them, is carried into their marital homes. There is a story of two brothers who engaged in a fight because they could not settle their differences and forgive each other. One day, the younger took a kitchen knife and stabbed the older in the neck, and he instantly bled to death.

The problem of unforgiveness and revenge has taken a lot of lives, destroyed many families and damaged so many marriages and relationships in our society today. Forgiveness in every relationship is a vital key to a successful, peaceful and lasting friendship. It was on this note that our Lord and Saviour Jesus Christ told us to pray daily for forgiveness. Our Lord's emphasis on forgiveness is apparent. He made it one of the prerequisites of going to heaven. You must forgive others if you want to go to heaven for only on the condition of you forgiving others will your sins be forgiven.

Unforgiveness is likened to a person who just drank poison and expects the other person to die. Unforgiveness causes a lot of problems including health challenges. Look at our society today, the killing on the streets by our youngsters. What are they dragging, not forgiving each other? That is why they are killing themselves. Unforgiveness is taking many precious lives from us. For us to be free and live a peaceful life, we need to forgive others. The disciples asked Jesus to teach them to pray. He taught them what we now call "Our Lord's Prayer" where forgiveness is a critical part.

The irony of unforgiveness is that the other person, most times, is not even aware that he or she has offended you. The person who did not forgive suffers more. Some sicknesses have been linked to unforgiveness, therefore teaching your children to learn to forgive is in other words, teaching them to live a healthy lifestyle from childhood. This may save their lives and their marriages in the future. When they learn to forgive, it will be of great benefit for them in the future even at workplaces and business. Forgiveness plays a significant role in keeping life and businesses alive and functioning very efficiently.

If you are a minister, you desperately need forgiveness. You cannot be successful in ministry if you do not forgive. Forgiveness is the keyword to learn because it protects lives and guarantees a peaceful home, and most of all you will have peace of mind.

Nuggets For Raising Godly Children

NUGGET 13

BE YOUR CHILD'S BEST FRIEND

Knowing your child or children is very important. In some families, parents are total strangers to their children and children are strangers to their parents, and it should not be like that. No matter how busy you claim to be, you must take time out to know who your child or children are and who they are growing to be. Do not wait for strangers to tell you who your children are. You need to know your children yourself. Every good parent should know who their children are, even to the point that you know when your child is telling lies or telling the truth. It is also vital the parents should know the movement of their children. It is unfortunate that lots of parents are too busy to know the whereabouts of their children. Sometimes you see children loitering on the street at odd hours, in their school uniforms, yet their parents are either at home busy or at work, not knowing their children are out, exposed to many dangerous and wicked people.

Some parents do not know their children's close friends or pals. Parents should know who their children's best friends and close pals are. It is with that knowledge that you can then advise your child whether or not to carry on with the friendship. I do know that so many children will object to their parent's advice, but it is imperative that parents should advise and say the truth which will set them free.

Whenever your children do something you are proud of, do not hesitate to appreciate them. Applaud them on every excellent achievement. So many parents are good with shouting at their children when they do wrong but do not compliment them when they do right. You need to balance your judgement. When our children get it wrong, we must correct them in love. Our children are watching our judgement; remember we are teaching them by the way we do things. If you do not applaud them on their achievement, but only criticise them on their wrong, this will confuse them on the difference between right and wrong, and between good and bad behaviour. This is because you never show them a positive response when they do right. Some married couples do not applaud each other when one does exceptionally well. They are always good with criticising their spouse when mistakes are made but certainly do not praise or appreciate each other when they have done something right. The reasoning is that they feel the partner if commended for their good may be puffed up and start behaving strangely. All these are strategies of the enemy to rob couples of the joy which they should derive from that accomplishment.

Parents should remember that your children are watching the way you behave with each other. You will be shocked that is what they will replicate in their own marital homes. Then you may be called to come and settle problems. Therefore, compliment your spouse when necessary, and treat each other very well so that your children will treat their spouse well — model good examples by being a good example yourself. You may be the Bible your children are reading to correct their ways. They learn by what they see and not necessarily by what you say to them.

> *"Wherefore I beseech you, be ye followers of me. For this cause have I sent unto you Timotheus, who is my beloved son, and faithful in the Lord, who shall bring you into remembrance of my ways which be in Christ, as I teach everywhere in every church" (1 Corinthians 4:16-17).*

Nuggets For Raising Godly Children

NUGGET 14

BUILD THEIR SELF-ESTEEM

God in His mercy gave you these children to look after. Among the billions of people in the whole world, He chose you to take care of these precious ones. I think you should consider yourself privileged for many are still waiting for their bundle of blessing.

For those who are waiting, let me relate to you the testimony I read of a couple who were married and trusted God for the fruit of the womb for seventeen years. Amazingly, after seventeen years of waiting, the good Lord blessed them with six children at the same time. So, there is hope for you my brother and my sister; keep trusting Him. He never fails and will never fail because of you, amen.

The children God gave you are innocent; they do not know anything. They depend on you to teach them what to do and where to go. Where you live is their home, and your people automatically become their people. Think about it, your children arrive with nothing, totally depending on you to guide them, show them the way and to give them a people to call their own. That means you have a great responsibility in your hands and a lot of people do not realise this. The job of building them up is in your hands.

We must realise that our children arrive in different forms and we need to take them all along. Some children are confident, while others have no confidence at all, and we must build up their confidence. It is our responsibility to build our children's self-confidence by empowering them with positive words; words of encouragement that will build them up, not the ones that will bring them down. Confidence is vital in the life of every child. It empowers them to grow to higher ground. The job of building your child's confidence is yours as a parent. Please do not allow others to do it for you; they might give them the wrong information or lead them the wrong direction. In all, they may not do a good job like you, especially if their motives are not right. You know rightly that no one will give what they do not have, so the people on the street will not have the right information to build up a child today positively. They can only give what they have, that is why many are falling prey on our streets today of the knife and gun crime because that is what the street can offer. Therefore, you do your best to carry out this job of building the child's confidence and self-esteem.

There is power in the spoken words. Every word you speak carry power and is alive. Our God created the world by the words of His mouth and created us in His image. Therefore, speak those words to your children, and they will live in them and build their confidence and self-esteem.

As children levels of confidence and understanding are different so also should the parents walk with them with that understanding. Understanding your child is paramount in guiding and building them up. Do not compare them with each other or with outsiders. Remember that whenever some children are misunderstood, their self-esteem lowers, and their confidence drops. Therefore, I will advise that as parents, we need to be mindful of our child's personality. Do your best to uplift the spirit of your children as this is vital. Any little encouragement to these precious little ones will go a long way to motivate them to do more and add more effort. Parents should always make an effort to inspire their children and praise them anytime they do something positive in life, or they make any accomplishment. This is very important for their growth, their development and their future.

Nuggets For Raising Godly Children

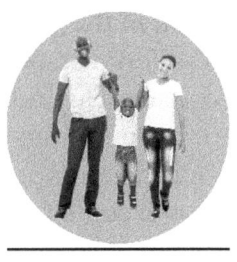

NUGGET 15

CREATE THEIR WORLD BY YOUR WORDS

Speak positive things into the lives of your children.

> "And God said, Let there be light: and there was light" (Genesis 1:3).

So, God created everything by the utterance of His mouth.

> "And God said, Let us make man in our image, after our likeness: and let them have dominion over the fish of the sea, and over the fowl of the air, and over the cattle, and over all the earth, and over every creeping thing that creepeth upon the earth" (Genesis 1:26).

And God made man in His image and after his likeness. We are made in the image of God. I want us to reflect on these few verses. God said things, and they happened just as He said. In the same way, He created us to make things happen by our utterances, which means we open our mouth and say things and they will come to pass.

In this context, I want to say that some children have missed their God-given purposes in life because of the utterances of their parents. It is vital as parents to watch what we say to our children. It is advisable that we say positive things to our children; confess creative things into their lives. We need to continually declare good things to our children and grandchildren because out of our mouth proceeds issues of life. A preacher once said "If you are not saying anything, you are not creating anything." Therefore, please say good things to your children. You need to understand the power in your utterances, make it a point of duty to always say something positive to your children. Remember, everything you say to your children and grandchildren either builds them up or destroys them. Do your best to make sure your words are creating a better future for the coming generation. Some of us forget so quickly that the babies we have in our hands today by the special grace of God will turn out to be the boys and girls of tomorrow even men and women who carry the future generation when we are gone. Positive words we speak to them and towards them go a long way to shape and build their future. Do your best to confess positive things to them and towards them. Please do not lay a curse on your children because it will happen. The children suffer it and their grandchildren, and it goes on until somebody breaks that curse.

There is a family whose grandfather laid a curse on their father's daughters regarding their marriage before he died. That curse affected those women. I saw the curse manifest and it was not pleasant. Please, parents, do not lay a curse on your children because God has given you authority over your children to guide them and lead them in the right direction. As always, bless them and do not curse them because they are your flesh and blood. Sometimes, parents do not mean to cause harm to their children, but the habit of saying negative things has become part of them. Let us try our best to control our emotions by making sure we always say positive things from our mouth.

On this note, if you think that there is a curse following you from your parents, either your mums' side or dads' side, please seek help immediately before it continues to the next generation. Please do not allow it to be passed to the next generation. You can speak to your mum or your dad for they have the history of your lineage before they are called home. Remember, blessing works as effective as curses work. So, bless and keep blessing your children. If you are reading this book and your parents are alive, please do follow these critical instructions. You know that, to your parents, you are still their baby boy or baby girl. So please, buy something special and visit them wherever they are, present the gifts to them, kneel in front of them and make this very important request from them – "Ask them to bless you."

Make sure this is done. It works. Isaac blessed his sons before he died.

> *"And Isaac called Jacob, and blessed him, and charged him, and said unto him, thou shalt not take a wife of the daughters of Canaan. Arise, go to Padan–aram, to the house of Bethuel thy mother's father; and take thee a wife from thence of the daughters of Laban thy mother's brother. And God Almighty bless thee, and make thee fruitful, and multiply thee, that thou mayest be a multitude of people; And give thee the blessing of Abraham, to thee, and to thy seed with thee; that thou mayest inherit the land wherein thou art a stranger, which God gave unto Abraham" (Genesis 28:1-4).*

NUGGET 16

MOTIVATE THEM TO AIM HIGH

Our children are the gift of God to us because they are our offsprings; we gave birth to them and are raising them. Therefore, we must inspire them to aim high in life. Great aspiration is engendered from childhood when the foundation is laid. It is the parent's responsibilities to challenge their children to reach for the stars. The ability to do so has been given to us by God who has entrusted them into our care. The power is in our hands to guide our children to higher ground. Being innocent, our children follow our guide especially if we guide them well.

> *"Children, obey your parents in the Lord: for this is right. Honour thy father and mother; which is the first commandment with promise; That it may be well with thee, and*

thou mayest live long on the earth" (Ephesian 6:1-3).

God has given every parent the power to do this job to the best of our abilities. This means we can raise them to be the best they can be. We can inspire them to achieve the highest standard in our society. It is possible, and many parents are achieving it already. Why would you think your children should achieve average or even lower than average, when others can make it to the top? You keep praying and keep talking to them making them understand that they can be the best in whatever it is they ever desire. The key is, having confidence and putting their faith in God Almighty. Then everything is possible.

Parents can challenge their children to take the bull by the horns and achieve the best. This we know is possible, not by nagging them but by inspiring them and motivating them with kind words which goes a long way to build them up to accomplish whatever they set their mind to.

> *"Jesus answered and said unto them, Verily I say unto you, If ye have faith, and doubt not, ye shall not only do this which is done to the fig tree, but also if ye shall say unto this mountain, Be thou removed, and be thou cast into the sea; it shall be done. And all things, whatsoever ye shall ask in prayer, believing, ye shall receive" (Matthew 21:21-22).*

In some cases, parents have helped their children in making positive choices in life. Some may not initially agree or cooperate, but most times, when parents assist their children in making their choices, they had yielded positive results. The decisions made by our children are vital to their future. Parents stand a better chance of influencing their children in the choices they make. We state facts and reasons we think they should make the best choices not because friends are making the same choices but the importance of those choices in the long run.

The daughter of a gentleman well known to me chose a career. Following three years of university study in a specific course, she graduated but could not get a job related to her chosen profession. She had to return to university to study another course which has now led her to the career that is currently putting food on her table and provide her with a better life.

Please, parents, have a say in the life choices your children are making. If your parents did not get involved in your decisions, you would not have achieved and accomplished what you have today. Please do not say it's their life and their choices. Remember, if it goes wrong, it will come back to you. My mum guided me, and that is why I am where I am today, still aiming high by the special grace of God.

"For with God nothing shall be impossible"
(Luke 1:37).

As a parent, you should be aware that if your children achieve well, it will be to their credit and advantage, and pride and joy to you. However, if your children did not do well, you will be concerned and grieved. You cannot throw a party when you see that your children did not do well. Instead, you would be running around to see if you can help them to remedy the situation and make them happy. Please do not wait until the end when you would be looking for a remedy.

Start getting involved early and play your part; they are your children so do your best because they deserve the best. Your best will be fine, so give them your best. Your best will help them to make the right choices in life. Your best will help them to act appropriately. Your best is while you are raising them, make them a priority. Your best is to invest in them. Your best is to spend time with them in order to correct and guide them. Your best is to do whatever you can and all it takes to help them succeed in life by the grace of God. Our good Lord will crown your efforts in Jesus name Amen. But remember that the race is not to the swift.

> *"I returned, and saw under the sun, that the race is not to the swift, nor the battle to the strong, neither yet bread to the wise, nor yet riches to men of understanding, nor yet favour to men of skill; but time and chance happeneth to them all" (Ecclesiastes 9:11).*

We must rely on God Almighty, pray to Him and trust our children into His mighty and powerful hands knowing that He will successfully take our children to their destination.

Everyone, including our children, have one life. Therefore, let us impact this generation. It will be so sad that we lived all the number of years the good Lord has given us in this world and fail to make an impact in the lives of people around us. It may be that you were not privileged enough to have the kind of opportunities our children are having, yet you got to where you are now. Please let us do our very best to make sure our children get the best and be the best in their time, and I am very sure you will be so proud of them and yourself as well.

Nuggets For Raising Godly Children

NUGGET 17

BE THE SHEPHERD AND NOT THE BULL

As a parent, all your conduct, lifestyle and behaviours are being watched by your children. You are the example your children see daily. Some parents are not as gentle as the shepherd of their children. Most times, the way the parents behave is the same way their children will act when they become adults themselves.

I remember the story of a family well known to me. The father of this house who is supposed to be the shepherd, the head and the priest of his family, decided to be the bull of the house instead. He abused and brutalised his wife and children, and there was constant domestic violence in their home, and the Police and Ambulances were called regularly. As these acts were going on, the children were watching, and the abuse was being registered in their memories. This confirms the proverbial saying, "Wherever two Elephants are fighting, it is the grass that suffers."

As parents are quarrelling and fighting, it is your children that are being subjected to emotional torture. What can the poor children do? Only to soak their pillows and beds with tears as they hear the curses, slaps and blows raining down from either mummy or daddy. It is not always a pleasant experience. Any child who has been through this will attest to this.

Back to my story. The man whom God has ordained to be the shepherd of the house turned into a bull. The marriage finally ended, and the lady took the children and continued to raise them in the way of the Lord. One day as this lady decided to visit the grandparents of the children, the grandfather knowing that their marriage has ended because domestic of violence, on seeing this lady and her children started weeping very uncontrollably. Everyone was shocked at that very act but were very curious to know what prompted this reaction. The grandfather began by apologising to the lady and her children for all they have been through claiming it was his fault. He said the actions and behaviour of his son were as a result of the way he behaved when he was living with his mum many years ago. He confessed he was ruthless and abusive, beating his wife and being very violent to the family as the head of the home. He apologised unreservedly saying that his son copied precisely the way he treated his mum. He also confessed that he never knew his son would grow up to replicate his lifestyle. He sobbed until the lady accepted his apologies.

When was the last time you took your son or daughter on a dad and son, mother and daughter walk, spoke to him or her in a sweet and lovely way? When was the last time you had family time together and talked, joked and laughed? In some homes, as soon as daddy or mummy arrive home, all the children must go to their rooms, so they are not disturbed. On approach some parents will start screaming and shouting, always finding faults and reason to make everyone very uncomfortable. Because he or she is the breadwinner, when they are at home, no one is comfortable; no happy time with the family.

Any parent doing this is a big bull of the home. Instead of being the shepherd and enjoying the lovely family our good Lord has granted you, you are bullish. Let me ask you, when will you enjoy your family? Is it when they are grown and gone out of your home? Please enjoy them now that you still have the opportunity. This period will never be forever. Cease from being the bull. Remember, they are watching your behaviour. The girls will do to their husband as they saw their mummy did to their daddy, and the boys will treat their wives the same way they saw their daddy handled their mother. You do not expect anything different. The saying is true; "What goes around comes around." So, please parents, sow good seed into the lives of your children by being the shepherd and watch it manifest as they grow in the Lord.

NUGGET 18

LEAVE THE INHERITANCE INSIDE YOUR CHILDREN

Parents and grandparents should endeavour to leave inheritance for their children. This is a godly act and has scriptural backing.

> *"A good man leaveth an inheritance to his children's children: and the wealth of the sinner is laid up for the just"* (Proverbs 13:22).

Pay close attention to this important word of wisdom. No matter how much material inheritance you leave for your children, it will not make them successful. What will make them successful is what you leave inside them. If you leave nothing inside them, whatever you leave outside as an inheritance will be squandered. A typical example is the Biblical Prodigal Son.

"And he said, A certain man had two sons: And the younger of them said to his father, Father, give me the portion of goods that falleth to me. And he divided unto them his living. And not many days after the younger son gathered all together, and took his journey into a far country, and there wasted his substance with riotous living. And when he had spent all, there arose a mighty famine in that land; and he began to be in want. And he went and joined himself to a citizen of that country, and he sent him into his fields to feed swine. And he would fain have filled his belly with the husks that the swine did eat: and no man gave unto him. And when he came to himself, he said, How many hired servants of my father's have bread enough and to spare, and I perish with hunger! I will arise and go to my father, and will say unto him, Father, I have sinned against heaven, and before thee, And am no more worthy to be called thy son: make me as one of thy hired servants. And he arose, and came to his father. But when he was yet a great way off, his father saw him, and had compassion, and ran, and fell on his neck, and kissed him. And the son said unto him, Father, I have sinned against heaven, and in thy sight, and am no more worthy to be called thy son. But the father said to his servants, Bring forth the best robe, and put it on him; and put a ring on his hand, and shoes on his feet: And bring hither the fatted calf, and kill it; and let us

eat, and be merry: For this my son was dead, and is alive again; he was lost, and is found. And they began to be merry" (Luke 15:11-24).

Because this boy has nothing inside of him to sustain the wealth, the inheritance he received from his father was wasted, and he ended up with only one option; to feed and dine with swine (pigs). It is imperative that you spend your time and money as parents to impact your children's lives and build them up in line with current reality and not fantasies. You need to educate them about the difference between being 'straight,' as a complete man or woman, and being a gay or lesbian. Parents need to teach their young children the benefit of being who God have created them to be as different from choosing what they want to be, along with the repercussion of disobedience. Tell your children the advantages and disadvantages of obedience and back it up with Scriptures.

Please do not allow your children to be empty or uninformed about vital information of life; otherwise, the devil will use his agents to fill them up and cause confusion in your home. Do not commit the training and equipping of your children solely to the Schools and the Sunday Schools. Do your job by teaching and keeping your children informed and our God will crown your effort with success.

Make sure you enrich your children inside. It is crucial if you want them to be successful in life.

Equip your children with wisdom, knowledge and understanding. If they ask you one question, it is a privilege. Use it as an opportunity to respond with godly answers including examples and references. This saying is vital at this point: "Instead of always giving a man fish, it is better to teach him how to fish so he will not bother you anymore."

Instead of making your children reliant on your wealth, why not teach them to work hard and smart to earn their wealth, so that they can be independent? Even if they take over your business empire, they need to first manage themselves. Otherwise, how can they control your empire? If they are rich inside, even if you leave your inheritance for them, you are rest assured that it is in good hands because they will make you proud of their success. But if they have nothing inside them, even if you leave billions of pounds for them, just as the prodigal son, it only takes a few bad friends who will entice them into clubbing, gambling, drugs or wrong investments and before you know it, all that wealth will be lost. If you leave precious wealth in the hand of an incompetent person, it's only a matter of time before everything will be gone.

Many parent's regrets in life have always been one thing; not spending enough time with their family. When you spend time with your children, you impact their life and prepare them for the future. Do your best to spend time with your children so you can enrich them inside which will then manifest outside. So many Children are walking around empty. They have nothing inside them; no wisdom, no knowledge, and no understanding, all because some of their parents are busy chasing money, buying or building houses to make them financially comfortable. Some of these children are roaming the streets carrying knives, guns and drugs, while some are busy smoking weeds and drugs in the name of enjoyment. Because they have nothing inside, the roadside agents find it easy to brainwash them into their merchandise. They tell them that right is wrong and wrong is right, and they believe it. Most of these children waste their lives and the lives of others because they have nothing inside them. So please, parents, spend time with your children and impact and enrich their lives inside instead of piling up treasure for them outside as inheritance.

Nuggets For Raising Godly Children

NUGGET 19

TEACH ABOUT FINANCIAL INTELLIGENCE

Teach your children to save and invest.

Too many parents think that if their children are denied anything, it means that they have failed in their responsibilities as good parents. Therefore, they go all the way to make sure their children have whatever they so desired. Buying your children whatever they wished is not bad but teaching them to save is vital, more especially when you show them how to invest which set them up for life. Today, most young people are not thinking of investing. Instead, they are involved in spending, even when their parents are on state benefits. Their focus is on the most expensive gadgets and accessories in vogue.

Teaching your children to invest is a critical part of raising them as godly children so that they will be self-supporting.

I remember one of our brethren who in the course of our discussion told me that his son in secondary school purchases cars from his pocket money and sells in his car shop. For me, it was mind-blowing for a sixteen-year-old boy to have such level of an investment idea. The father taught him from early about savings and investment.

Starting early is vital so that by the time they grow up, their mindset is shaped up and before you know it they will be financially free while their mates are still struggling to feed themselves. A great man once said; "if you take all the money in the world, and share it into equally to everyone, in few years, the rich will be rich while the poor will remain poor. It's all a matter of their mindset." The reason is that most poor people are always having a consumer mindset while the rich have an investment mindset. Show me a poor man and I will show you a person who "Passes Over Opportunities Repeatedly" (POOR).

Investment mindset is developed when you are young. Most millionaires grabbed it at a very young age through their mindset apart from those that inherited wealth. Please prepare the mindset of your children by making a start with creating a bank account for them. You may start with the Piggybank. As soon as they receive money, teach them to save and not to consume all. Gradually you will see that the saving mindset will spring in. You can only invest what you have, only when the money is there. Teach them small. Rome was not built in a day. Parents should also learn to invest as this will encourage their young child to do likewise; invest in properties, shares, bonds, etc. Many people fear investment. It is a way of life. Once you cultivate it into the experience of your children, it will never leave them. Instead, it will multiply and increase to the point that they will have to teach and help others to do the same.

Nuggets For Raising Godly Children

NUGGET 20

TEACH THEM TO COOK

"Train up a child in the way he should go: and when he is old, he will not depart from it" (Proverbs 22:6).

Cooking is a significant part of life, whether male or female; the house chores is for everyone especially where there is understanding in a family. It is vital that parents should teach their children how to cook their meals. Occasional eating out (and take out) is advisable but not all the time. Every family house has a place called the kitchen, where food is prepared, so parents should teach their children to make use of that part of the house too. There will be a time in life when a child will be on his or her own, either in the University, as a spinster, bachelor or living alone as a single person in their own house or flat. At a period when you are not there with them, they will need to make use of the kitchen and make their food. If all these while he or she has not been into the kitchen except to go and pick his or her food and eat, and never learn to cook his or her meal, then we have not done well on that part, and it will be challenging to start late in life.

A lady told me a story of the first vegetable soup she made when growing up, which did not turn out very well. She was born into a wealthy family with servants all around her. Her mum insisted she learns how to cook. This lady in question cooked the soup, and it was bitter. So, the mum instructed her to continue eating that soup until it finished. Through the process of repetitive practice, she mastered how to cook.

You could not blame your daughter in her husband's house if you get a complaint that she cannot cook well if you did not find the time to teach her how to cook even your native delicacies.

Let us balance this by taking out time to teach our children how to cook; they cannot continue eating noodles and boiled eggs forever. On the other hand, some people would not mind eating out all the time, maybe because they have the money to foot the bill. That may not be for everyone. Therefore, teaching children to cook is very important.

A young lady thought she does not need to learn how to cook. Her dear mother called her several times to come to learn how to prepare even the simple African 'Jollof Rice' dish or vegetable soup, but she said, "oh mum don't worry yourself, I will marry a rich man and we will not need to cook, we will always eat out." After secondary school, she gained admission to a remote countryside University. Now leaving on her own, after the first semester, the food the mum made for her ran out. She started to spend her upkeep money on take away food. Realising that she was running low on money, she quickly located the nearest supermarket and started asking mum how to prepare Jollof Rice. Her mum gladly guided her. Unfortunately for her, as she got to the shop, she suddenly realised that there were about six different types of rice. Which one does she buy? She had to call the mum again to ask which one she should buy. Mum gracefully guided her. She wanted to buy tomatoes, there were different types, and she called again. Thank God for video call as mum was kind to take her through the buying process. Now to cook the food, she called mum to know when to put the rice, what to do next and next. Just then the mum said to her, "you can consult Mr Google to help you out. I can't help you anymore." She used YouTube to complete her cooking.

The children may use the skill or not but let us teach them. No knowledge is a waste. Therefore, let us show them the right thing and allow them to make their own decision.

Nuggets For Raising Godly Children

NUGGET 21

LOVE YOUR CHILDREN UNCONDITIONALLY

Love is a four-letter word but very powerful and essential in all areas of life. In the family, love is the keyword that takes them to their expectation. Every couple starts with love for each other. My wife and I started with love. God in His grace then blessed us with children whom we love so dearly, yet still, love each other. As the children grow, we must practically demonstrate to them that we love them by providing for them and correcting them in love. We need not allow our children to carry on doing the wrong things in order not to offend them or upset them, and when the consequences come, it falls back on us.

I do think genuine love is the love that saves, which leads to eternal life. This type of love was demonstrated by our Father in heaven who sent us Jesus Christ our Lord and Saviour.

> *"For God so loved the world, that he gave his only begotten Son, that whosoever believeth in him should not perish, but have everlasting life" (John 3:16).*

This sacrificial love brought us salvation. If Christ did not sacrifice His life and go through pain and agony, how could we have made it? He sacrificed His pleasure so that we should have eternal life.

Our children should also experience this love through us. We should teach them the love of God by loving them with all our heart and be there to sacrifice in order for them to achieve excellence in life. I want to use this opportunity to congratulate those parents who have made various sacrifices (and continue to do so) towards their children which is making significant impact in the lives of their children. I can only say well done, and God will bless you and keep you to enjoy the fruit of your labour in Jesus name, Amen.

Love your children enough to tell them the truth even if it offends them. That truth will in return set them free in the end. Do not feel intimidated even if your children appear to be bigger than you such that you fear to correct and tell them the truth.

Eli the Prophet did not correct his children and tell them the truth of the consequences of their actions based on what the scripture said. Even when God warned them through young Samuel, Eli did not rebuke them. He knew that calamity was coming, yet he did not bother. What can I say to that account, the result was that they all died on the same day which spelt doom for the whole nation of Israel.

> *"And the Lord said to Samuel, Behold, I will do a thing in Israel, at which both the ears of everyone that heareth it shall tingle. In that day I will perform against Eli all things which I have spoken concerning his house: when I begin, I will also make an end. For I have told him that I will judge his house for ever for the iniquity which he knoweth; because his sons made themselves vile, and he restrained them not. And therefore, I have sworn unto the house of Eli, that the iniquity of Eli's house shall not be purged with sacrifice nor offering for ever" (1 Sumuel 3:11-14).*

As a Christian parent, start demonstrating this godly love from your home. Some Christian parents are saints in the church and are something different at home. The truth of the matter is that your children should taste and enjoy your love first before you take it outside. The Christian life is a practical lifestyle; you cannot hide it. The scripture said a house built on the hill cannot be hidden, neither do men lit a candle and put it under a basket.

"Ye are the light of the world. A city that is set on an hill cannot be hid. Neither do men light a candle, and put it under a bushel, but on a candlestick; and it giveth light unto all that are in the house. Let your light so shine before men, that they may see your good works, and glorify your Father which is in heaven" (Mathew 5:14-16).

Please show your children, practical love, just as our saviour Jesus is our example. Everybody can feel love. When you are loved, you know it. Letting your children feel your love should not stop you from correcting them in that same spirit of love. Do not love them so much to the point that you cannot correct nor discipline then if necessary. That is not loving. Please love them and correct and discipline them when they do wrong. Try your best as parents to keep the balance so that your children will be the best for themselves and you.

NUGGET 22

DISCIPLINE AND CORRECT YOUR CHILDREN IN LOVE

The word of God teaches,

"Train up a child in the way he should go: and when he is old, he will not depart from it" (Proverbs 22:6).

"He that spareth his rod hateth his son: but he that loveth him chasteneth him betimes" (Proverbs 13:24).

"Foolishness is bound in the heart of a child; but the rod of correction shall drive it far from him" (Proverbs 22:15).

There are other scriptural backings for correcting your children in a godly and lovely way so that you will get the best result out of your children. There is no one way in which one can say this is the best and only way a child can be corrected, but each child should be corrected with love at heart. When correcting a child, you should have love in your mind, whether you are using the old method or the modern way of correcting your child, please remember they are children and are naïve.

We are privileged to be here at this 21st century where everything does not depend on your physical power, nor your strength. Today, things are not the same. The 21st century is a time when we can apply the Scripture in different ways depending on the state of the mind of your child. In order to get the best result, the 'rod' in the scripture may not mean the physical rod by application in our time; it may be the gargets, TV time, play time, the toy or anything that will make the child think and reflect on what has just happened. You may consider time out or a corner stand or anything you will deprive that child that will be as effective as the rod of correction, which will make the child react positively and obey your good instructions. The law of the land is changing speedily and smacking or flogging a child, or any human being is outlawed.

As Christians, we must be obedient to the laws of the land so that we will not lose the privilege of training our children in a godly way to the state. Many parents have disobeyed this part of the law and have seen themselves in trouble with the law. Many have even lost their children to social services. Some also went to prison in the name of correcting or disciplining their children. Our children are classified by law as vulnerable and defenceless, so when you are correcting them, you must bear in mind that they need to be protected by you even amid that correction. Otherwise, it may be classified as abuse.

Your children depend on you for their protection. They trust you because God has given them over to you. Remember, not everyone has the grace to take care of a child, so whenever an opportunity comes your way, please make great use of it.

Every parent is rest assured of their child's trust and reliability. They have faith in you and believe that you will not hurt them. But in some cases, parents have disappointed the little ones to the point that the government have had to step in to defend these defenceless children. Alarmingly, we have witnessed some children dying in the hands of their parents and guardians all in the name of discipline and correction.

At this point, I must point out that you can win more with love than hate. Correction made in love will never hurt or kill. Therefore, let us apply wisdom and correct our children in love knowing that they are precious before the Lord. Someone may wonder, to what extent can a child be corrected or disciplined? Yes, to the extent that the child is safe. Remember the reason for correction and discipline is to save the future of this child, but some parents on the contrary abuse their children in the process of correcting and disciplining them thereby ending up ruining the future of these children.

Knowing your child is very important in this context. If you have raised that child from birth until now, you will know the appropriate disciplinary step that will suit your child that will make the child listen to and obey you. All you want is for your child to listen to and obey you and for your child's future to be great. Always hold God at His word in prayer, lifting all your children by name before Him daily.

Whenever a child did not receive adequate discipline and correction, the child feels left out. Some parents may disagree with me but since I have experienced growing up without a dad, I do know what it means to grow without discipline and correction. Growing up, whenever I saw fathers advising or correcting their children of my age, I will leave whatever I am doing and pay attention because I did not have someone to speak to me in that manner.

There was a case of a young man in my area whose Mum and Dad did not give adequate correction and discipline. He started with stealing meat from the pot and graduated to pick-pocketing the parents. He then joined a gang and from there graduated to armed robbery. When he was caught and sentenced to death by firing squad at their local village square, his last wish was to whisper something to his mother. At close contact, he bit off the mother's ear. When asked why he did that, he said his parents, particularly his mother, was the reason he was dying the shameful untimely death because she did not discipline and correct him when he started stealing meat from the pot of stew.

Discipline and correction are vital in raising godly children.

Nuggets For Raising Godly Children

NUGGET 23

'NO' IS A GODLY ANSWER

'No' is an answer with no scriptural basis but it is imperative in raising godly children. Our God does not always say 'yes' to all our requests. If He does, we will all be spoilt and may not have our due respect for Him. To some of our requests, He says 'no.' Why is it then difficult for us to sensibly and reasonably say 'no' to our children? There are three ways our God answers prayers:

1) He says 'yes,' and give us our hearts desires and requests.

2) He says 'wait it is not yet time to have it,' and in due time He releases our blessings and answers our requests.

3) He says 'no,' and the request is never answered.

With these three principles of God answering our prayers which are practised in our time, why do we not apply them in raising our children instead of saying 'yes' to all their requests?

I remember my son-in-the-Lord. Immediately after his conversion and follow-up, he wanted to embark on some days of dry fast and prayers concerning a situation to which he wanted God to respond. I did my best to discourage him and asked him to pray and to ask God to answer if it is His will. He thankfully followed my advice and did not embark on that programme the way he planned it. Today, this my son is still in the Lord and is now an ordained minister of the gospel and doing so well in the Lord. Our God is merciful, but he is Almighty.

God is in charge; the whole world belongs to him. He cannot be ordered around, pushed about or moved by our instructions. Concerning my son-in-the-Lord, if God did not answer his request with a 'yes', it would have discouraged him and today, he may no longer be in the faith.

Therefore, it is vital for us to help our children to get used to the answer 'no' so that if it comes from any corner, they can handle it and they will not create problems to you. As they grow to the age of building relationships, if their proposals are rejected or their expectations are not met, some may feel suicidal because they are not used to the 'no' response. Please teach them to accept 'no' as an answer and move on. Sometimes saying 'no' will close one door and will lead to another door being opened better than the first one.

Saying 'no' to our children does not make us wicked parents as many of us may presume. Many children may not be able to handle it if we say 'no' to their request. If we always say 'yes' to our children without a 'no,' then there is not a balance and may create the impression to them that everything is possible. But let us learn to say 'no' sometimes to create a balance, otherwise in the future, if we say 'no' it will create a fuss. It may later become a problem especially in letting them have their way and do their own thing and not interfering. Please, deliberately refuse to let them have everything they ask. It will go a long way to teach them a lot in life. The 'no' you say today may save their life tomorrow and secure their future.

Let us try to balance our children's understanding; that they cannot have everything they want. Even when you can afford it, please do not make it available so that they will appreciate what you have provided for them and respect you for doing that as their parents. God bless you as you appropriate this accordingly.

Nuggets For Raising Godly Children

NUGGET 24

KEEP THEM ALWAYS BEFORE THE THRONE

You must keep speaking to God on your children's behalf. If you are reading this book and your child has wandered away for a while now, out of God's presence, please keep speaking to God on their behalf. Do not stop praying because it keeps the fire burning. So long the fire keeps burning, it keeps the wolves away. The wolf of stealing, the wolf of death, and that of destruction; these are the three-primary assignment of the devil. He is the wolf. He only comes for three reasons, to steal, to kill and to destroy. While you are busy talking to God about them, God will through His word keep the wolf away from them.

The story of the prodigal son is a clear example.

"And he arose, and came to his father. But when he was yet a great way off, his father saw him, and had compassion, and ran, and fell on his neck, and kissed him. And the son said unto him, Father, I have sinned against heaven, and in thy sight, and am no more worthy to be called thy son. But the father said to his servants, Bring forth the best robe, and put it on him; and put a ring on his hand, and shoes on his feet: And bring hither the fatted calf, and kill it; and let us eat, and be merry: For this my son was dead, and is alive again; he was lost, and is found. And they began to be merry" (Luke 15:20-24).

While the boy was away, the father was still expectant of his return. Considering the father's background, he might have been praying for help to build such a strong faith that he kept looking out expecting his son's return. The father of the prodigal did two significant things; praying and watching. That was why when he showed up the father recognised from a distance and ran to embrace him, welcomed him home and make merry on his behalf.

When parents pray for their children, God answers. Remember He gave those children to you.

"Lo, children are an heritage of the Lord: and the fruit of the womb is his reward" (Psalm 127:3).

Having the understanding that the child is a gift from God, we have to always communicate with God concerning the gift He gave to us. He is the maker. Just as every maker of a product have a solution when things go wrong, and the manufacturers have the answer to every problem, so is God the father.

Nuggets For Raising Godly Children

NUGGET 25

PRAY FOR YOUR FUTURE IN-LAWS

The next line of prayers may not make sense to so many, but it is vital for the joy, happiness and fulfilment of our children. We need to start praying for our children's future spouses. I tell you the truth; this one is very effective. Do you know that when you are making this prayer, you are praying for your future? If you have a loving and kind son or daughter-in-law, you are the one to enjoy the fringe benefits. Some parents are blessed with only female (or male) children according to how it pleases the Lord to share His blessings. The in-laws turn out to fill the gap and take care of them. If the reverse is the case, and the son or daughter-in-law are uncaring, it spells disaster. Sometimes they introduce their spouse to drugs or crime that may even lead them to an early grave.

Parents need to pray that God will guide their children to the right life partners. I do believe that God has prepared people for each other, and it takes His guidance to connect them. When you pray for them, God will do the rest by linking them up or making their paths to cross. The right spouse meant for them from above will locate them or they will locate whoever it may be and wherever they may be. Both will live the rest of their happy lives together.

ABOUT THE BOOK

This book is aimed at equipping parents, parents-to-be, grandparents and guardians in raising godly children in this sinful, wicked and adulterous generation. This book is also aimed at directing our children towards the Almighty God our creator through our Savour Jesus Christ. The lack of the fear of God in our generation is the actual reason for the violence we see daily in our time. This has resulted in the unnecessary killing of innocent young people. It sounds like no one is safe anymore. Hardly any day goes by that you will not hear of another person either shot dead or knifed down and in critical condition. How long will this last? It is in attempting to answer some of these questions that this book which was conceived inside me for the past fifteen years is birthed. Following the development and current situation of things today, it pleased the good Lord for me to pen down the things that could be the contributing factors and information that can bring a solution if adhered to, as we move to the next generation.

Scripture said in Psalms 11:3,

> *"If the foundations be destroyed, what can the righteous do?"*

It is a known fact that most violence is a direct result of the wrong foundation, which has informed the upbringing of these children. This book is a guiding tool to parents, as they prepare to start a family including the grandparents to be also. It is essential that we are not ignorant of 'The Last Days.'

Nuggets for Raising Godly Children in the sinful world starts with advising parents and parents-to-be on what to do from conception of a baby till the child is born; and instructions on how to raise the child in the way that will be pleasing to the Lord and the benefits to both the parents and children. How to build your child's self-esteem and self-confidence is another integral part of this book which prepares your children for the future. This book is aimed towards equipping everyone who spends their time to read and apply the principles mapped out in it for the purpose of enriching our younger generation in fulfilling their God-given plans and purposes in life.

It is very important to note that this book is aimed at achieving great result because our God never fails and in this case, I have full confidence that He who started this good work in our families by placing this book in your hand will fulfil it to a successful end in Jesus name Amen. God bless you.

ABOUT THE AUTHOR

Israel Ejiofor Philip is a pastor at the Right Now Jesus Centre, Elim Pentecostal Church, Rushey Green in Catford, Lewisham, London. He is married to Mrs Peace Nkeiruka Philip, and they are blessed with three children, Favour, Prince-Joseph and Israel Philip Junior. In 2003, Pastor Israel became the General Sunday School Superintendent of the Elim Pentecostal Church Camberwell and group of six Churches including the headquarters, which were later narrowed down to Rushey Green and Harlesden branches. Pastor Israel was a Sunday School Teacher in Nigeria, teaching both adult and children Sunday Schools before he relocated to the United Kingdom.

This book is a result of his years of experience with diverse classes of Sunday school children from different ethnic origins and race. His role as a Sunday School Superintendent availed him the opportunity to reach out to various sets of people and he has graduated over one hundred children (100) from the Sunday school into the youth and adult church and every child that passes through the Sunday School has an experience and a testimony of Salvation to the glory of God.

Pastor Israel just completed his Master of Science Degree in Counselling and Therapy with Atlantic Coast Theological Seminary, Florida. He has a Post

Graduate Certificate from the University of Wales England on Missional Theology. He completed his BSc. with Carolina University, USA. He had his diploma with South London Christian College.

Pastor Israel is an Evangelist by calling and operates in both the Evangelistic and Pastoral offices. He has a passion for soul-winning and feels fulfilled whenever a soul is worn into the Kingdom of God especially the young ones.

He believes passionately in Ecclesiastes 12:1 which says,

> *"Remember now thy Creator in the days of thy youth, while the evil days come not, nor the years draw nigh, when thou shalt say, I have no pleasure in them."*

www.ingramcontent.com/pod-product-compliance
Lightning Source LLC
Chambersburg PA
CBHW071516040426
42444CB00008B/1674